SUPERHEROES OF THE UNITED STATES CONSTITUTION

Superheroes of the United States Constitution

A Kid's Guide to American History Heroes

Written by
J. M. Bedell
Illustrated by
Bill Greenhead

Sky Pony Press books may be purchased in bulk at special discounts for sales promotion, corporate gifts, fund-raising, or educational purposes. Special editions can also be created to specifications. For details, contact the Special Sales Department, Sky Pony Press, 307 West 36th Street, 11th Floor, New York, NY 10018 or info@skyhorsepublishing.com.

Visit our website at www.skyhorsepublishing.com.

10 9 8 7 6 5 4 3 2 1

Library of Congress Cataloging-in-Publication Data
is available on file.

Cover design by Kai Texel
Cover and interior artwork: Bill Greenhead

ISBN: 978-1-5107-6777-5
eISBN: 978-1-63158-712-2

Printed in China

This book was previously published as *Superheroes of the Constitution* (ISBN: 978-1-63158-233-2)

CONTENTS

SUPERHEROES OF THE CONSTITUTION:

An Introduction

The Constitution of the United States of America was an experiment. No one knew whether it would fail or succeed. Could the people govern themselves without a king? Could thirteen separate colonies join and form a new nation? Could one Constitution set the rule of law for everyone and for all time? A lot of people said no.

But a whole lot more, including the ones you will meet in this book, said yes! And they set out to prove it. They risked their lives, the lives of their families, and everything they owned. None thought the cost too high, if, when the fight was over, they could live free.

The Constitution was designed to be the foundation for all law in the United States. It established how the government would function and what it could and could not do. It also recognized the rights of individuals and made sure no one could take those rights away.

There were times when the people wanted to change the Constitution. To do it, they had to get an *amendment* (correction) passed. That process wasn't easy. But it was designed that way. If it were easy, then a small number of people could force their will onto others. It takes the will of a lot of people to pass an amendment through both houses of Congress and get it *ratified* (approved) by three-fourths of the states.

Less than one hundred years after the Constitution was written, it was tested to its limits. The Civil War was tearing the nation apart. President Abraham Lincoln wondered whether the nation could survive. On November 19, 1863, on the battlefield at Gettysburg, he said,

> "Four score and seven years ago our fathers brought forth on this continent, a new nation, conceived in Liberty, and dedicated to the proposition that all men are created equal . . . [and] we here highly resolve . . . that this nation, under God, shall have a new birth of freedom—and that government of the people, by the people, for the people, shall not perish from the earth."

The nation did survive. It grew and changed, and the Constitution grew and changed with it. The men and women in this book are superheroes. They rose to the challenge of building a free nation and faced the injustices of their time. Their sacrifices and the sacrifices of hundreds of thousands more are what continue to make the United States of America a more perfect union!

Since the Constitution was first written, it has been amended twenty-seven times.

THE FREEDOM LEAGUE:

Creating a New Nation

The story of our Constitution begins when our nation was made up of thirteen colonies. We lived under the rule of King George III of Great Britain and his *parliament* (government). In the mid-1700s, Great Britain tried to collect more money from the colonies. They did it by putting new taxes on things like paper, sugar, and tea.

The colonists got mad, and they refused to pay. One day in 1773, Samuel Adams and his Sons of Liberty organization boarded three ships in Boston Harbor. They threw 342 chests of tea overboard. The colonists celebrated what was later called the Boston Tea Party. But the king didn't think it was funny. He punished the colonies by issuing new, stricter laws, what many came to call the Intolerable Acts. When the colonists complained, he refused to listen.

FIRST CONTINENTAL CONGRESS—SEPTEMBER 5 TO OCTOBER 26, 1774

In 1774, the leaders of the colonies decided it was time to take a stand. Each colony sent their best men to Carpenter's Hall in Philadelphia to form the First Continental Congress. Their plan was to ask the king to change his mind and end the new laws and taxes.

One of the men who attended that Congress was Patrick Henry from Virginia. He wanted the colonies to revolt against the king, and he was good at stirring up emotions!

Colonists threw tea overboard to protest the King's taxes.

LIBERTY or DEATH!
INTOLERABLE ACTS

PATRICK HENRY

(1736–1799)

Voice of the Revolution

Patrick Henry was born in in Virginia. He went to school for a while, but finished his education with a tutor at home.

He married Sarah Shelton and they lived on a three-hundred-acre farm that was a gift from Sarah's father. When the farm failed, Henry became a lawyer. He earned a reputation for being a powerful speaker. He argued that only the colonies, not the king or the parliament, had the right to collect taxes from the people. **The words he spoke and the strength of his belief stirred discontent among the colonists. He quickly became a leader of the protests against British rule.**

In 1774, Henry served as a *delegate* (representative) to the First Continental Congress. He helped write a *petition* (request) to the king asking to repeal the laws and taxes that were being forced on

As a child, Patrick Henry enjoyed playing the fiddle and the flute.

the colonies. The king ignored the petition. But Henry continued to stir up the people against the king. In 1775, he spoke at the Second Virginia Convention. Words from his speech lit the fire of revolution. He said,

> "Our brethren are already in the field! Why stand we here idle? . . . Is life so dear, or peace so sweet, as to be purchased at the price of chains and slavery? Forbid it, Almighty God! I know not what course others may take; but as for me, **give me liberty, or give me death!"**

During and after the Revolutionary War, Henry served as the first governor of Virginia and helped write that state's constitution. When President George Washington sent him a copy of the newly drafted Constitution, he thought it gave the federal government too much power and stomped on the rights of the states and the people. Henry's criticism was very important. His ideas led to many of the amendments that were later put into the Bill of Rights.

When the colonial leaders learned that the king was ignoring their pleas, they knew it was time to stand up and fight. But the people living in the colonies were divided. Some wanted to stay loyal to the king. Others would accept only revolution. Tensions were high. Everyone knew that war against the king was treason. If the colonies lost, many good men would face a firing squad or hang. The stakes were very high.

British troops marched into Lexington, Massachusetts, on April 19, 1775. They were there to enforce the king's laws. When they reached the village green, they were greeted by seventy minutemen. Someone fired the first shot. It isn't clear whether it

THE MINUTEMEN!

Minutemen were well-trained volunteer members of the militia. They had to keep their weapons with them and be ready to fight at a minute's notice.

was a British soldier or an American minuteman. When the chaos ended, eight colonists were dead. Word spread quickly through Boston and then through all the colonies. That shot made one thing very clear: the American Revolution had begun.

SECOND CONTINENTAL CONGRESS—MAY 10, 1775 TO MARCH 1, 1781

The Second Continental Congress met in the spring of 1775, after the historic battle at Lexington. This group of men would manage the war and begin to form a new government. Many of the men who had served in the First Continental Congress were part of the second.

One of their first acts was to write a formal Declaration of Independence. A team of five men was chosen to work on it. Thomas Jefferson, a man known for his great writing, was asked to write the first draft.

TIMOTHY MATLACK!

The original Declaration of Independence was handwritten by Timothy Matlack (1736–1826), a man with wonderful penmanship! It was written on parchment (animal skin treated with lime and stretched) so that the document would be strong and last a long time.

We the People
THWACK

THOMAS JEFFERSON

(1743–1826)

Father of the Declaration of Independence and Third President of the United States

Thomas Jefferson was born in Virginia. He loved to play the violin and read books. After college, he became a lawyer. He won many of his cases and became famous throughout Virginia. In 1772, he married Martha Skelton and they settled into their home at Monticello.

In 1776, as a delegate to the Second Continental Congress, Jefferson wrote the first draft of the Declaration of Independence in seventeen days. **Jefferson wrote words that forever changed the way people think. He said that people were born with certain rights and they should expect their government to work to protect them**. This was a radical idea at the time. He wrote:

"We hold these truths to be self-evident, that all men are created equal, that they are endowed by their Creator with certain unalienable Rights, that among these are Life, Liberty and the pursuit of Happiness."

The Declaration was approved on July 4, 1776, about one year after the start of the Revolutionary War.

Jefferson later served as a member of the Virginia House of Delegates, as governor of Virginia, and in the new Confederation Congress. In 1796, he was selected as the Republican candidate for president. He lost the race to John Adams by three

votes, which meant he had to serve a four-year term as Adam's vice president. In 1800, he ran again and was elected the third president of the United States. His election was the first time in history when one political party peacefully transferred power to another. He easily won a second term in 1804.

In his final years, Jefferson oversaw the construction of the nation's first non-religious university, the University of Virginia. He died on July 4, 1826, exactly fifty years after the signing of the Declaration of Independence.

Although Thomas Jefferson is credited with writing much of the lofty wording of the Declaration of Independence, fifty-six men signed it. But the person most closely associated with signing the legendary document was John Hancock.

Thomas Jefferson loved books and collected almost 6,500 of them. When the Library of Congress burned to the ground in 1841, he donated his collection to start a new library.

John Hancock

JOHN HANCOCK

(1737–1793)

Patriot of the American Revolution, First Signer of the Declaration of Independence, and First Governor of Massachusetts

John Hancock was born and raised in Massachusetts and attended Harvard. As a young adult, he worked in his uncle's successful shipping business, which he later inherited. He became a wealthy man and took on political positions in Boston and in the colonial legislature.

Because of his shipping business, Hancock was drawn into the growing revolt against Britain's taxation policies and other restrictions. He came into conflict with the British when his merchant ship, the *Liberty*, was seized in Boston Harbor. The British claimed that Hancock had not paid the required taxes on his imports. Because Hancock was an influential person in the city, the seizure of his ship led to protests by local residents.

After the Boston Massacre in 1770, when British soldiers fired their weapons into a group of unarmed citizens, **Hancock led the cry demanding that the British forces leave the city.** He also helped organize protests against the Tea Act. For these and other acts, **he was considered a major rabble-rouser by the British government**. In response, he used his wealth and in-

fluence to promote the movement for independence.Hancock was a delegate to the Second Continental Congress in 1775. As president of the Congress, he was the first person to sign the Declaration of Independence on July 4, 1776. **His signature was large with an unmistakable flourish. After that, the expression "leaving one's John Hancock"—signing a document—was coined.**

From 1780 to 1785, Hancock served as the first governor of Massachusetts. He was elected to a second term in 1787 and was the third governor of Massachusetts until his death in 1793.

Another signer of the Declaration of Independence was Samuel Adams. He had spent years in Boston advocating for independence from the king and organizing resistance to the British. He worked tirelessly to see his vision—of a society's right to govern itself—realized.

John Hancock's legacy continues in Boston's historic John Hancock building, the tallest building in the city and home to the John Hancock insurance company.

NO TAXATION
WITHOUT
REPRESENTATION

SAMUEL ADAMS

(1722–1803)

Leader of the American Revolution and Signer of the Declaration of Independence

Samuel Adams was born in Boston in 1722. He became involved in politics as a young adult, serving in the assembly. Adams launched a newspaper in 1748, called the *Independent Advertiser*. The paper was devoted entirely to politics, and Adams wrote most of the articles and letters to the editor. In the paper **he said that every society had the unquestionable right to govern itself**. He talked tirelessly about politics and devoted himself to local political gatherings. **An outspoken opponent of British rule, he wrote persuasive letters to the Boston newspapers and recruited many talented men to the Patriot cause.**

Adams's political ideas found an outlet when the British passed the Sugar Act in 1764. He became one of the first people to protest the act as taxation without representation and began to organize political action. The Sugar Act was repealed before Adams could get most of his plans off the ground. But the following year, when the British Parliament passed the Stamp Act, he was ready. He organized large protests. Because of his passionate persuasion, he became the leader of the resistance. When he was elected to the Massachusetts Assembly in 1766, **he used his position to rile British officials and encourage resistance.** When the Tea Act was passed, he helped plan the Boston Tea Party in protest.

At the First Continental Congress, he was one of the first to start advocating for independence from the British. He continued to work behind the scenes preparing campaigns of public resistance. Finally, his life's work triumphed when, in 1776, as a delegate to the Second Continental Congress, he signed the Declaration of Independence. Also signing was his younger cousin, John Adams, who would go on to become the second president of the United States.

TREATY OF PARIS—1783

Although the British had surrendered on October 19, 1781, British soldiers continued to occupy New York City. So the Confederation Congress sent Benjamin Franklin, John Jay, and John Adams to Paris, France, to negotiate with Great Britain. The king was forced to recognize American independence. In return, the United States would stop punishing people living in the states who had been loyal to the king and agreed to restore their property that had been taken during the war. This document became known as the Treaty of Paris and was signed on September 3, 1783. The last British troops finally left New York City on November 25, 1783.

The Treaty of Paris
ZZZZFNK!

BENJAMIN FRANKLIN
(1706–1790)
Author of the Treaty of Paris, Scientist, and Statesman

Benjamin Franklin was born in Boston and was the tenth child in a family of seventeen children. His father was a soap and candle maker. As a boy, Franklin worked in his father's shop. He had very little schooling, but luckily he was incredibly smart. When he wasn't working, he taught himself to read and write.

At the age of twelve, his father sent him to live and work for his older brother James. James was a printer and the founder of the first independent newspaper in America, the *New England Courant*. Franklin worked long hours writing pamphlets, setting type, and selling printed material in the streets of Boston.

Franklin loved to write, but his brother refused to print any of his work. Instead, Franklin secretly wrote fourteen essays under the name Silence Dogood. They were popular and James pub-

THE PENNSYLVANIA GAZETTE

lished every one. When he found out that Silence Dogood was Franklin, he was very angry.

Franklin left his apprenticeship and moved to Philadelphia, where he became a printer in his own right. He published *The Pennsylvania Gazette* and his most popular pamphlet, *Poor Richard's Almanack*. By the age of forty-two he was a wealthy man.He served in the colonial legislature and as postmaster for Philadelphia and then all the colonies. He became a member of the Continental Congress and served on the committee that drafted the Declaration of Independence. A short time later, he traveled to France, where he was considered a fashion icon and was popular with the ladies. While in France he **helped negotiate the Treaty of Paris, which ended the Revolutionary War.**

Benjamin Franklin was the only man who signed the Declaration of Independence, the Treaty of Alliance with France that promised mutual military support, the Treaty of Paris, and the United States Constitution.

In 1790, Franklin sent a petition to Congress asking for an end to slavery in the United States, but he died before seeing that happen.

The Treaty of Paris had other important conditions besides ending the war. The team of Benjamin Franklin, John Adams, and John Jay also secured fishing rights for the colonies in waters that belonged to Great Britain. And the king was forced to cede (give up) territory to the new country, vastly expanding its size.

Benjamin Franklin invented bifocal eyeglasses, the Franklin stove, wooden swimming fins, the odometer, and the lightning rod.

JOHN ADAMS

(1735–1826)

Drafter of the Declaration of Independence and the Treaty of Paris, Second President of the United States

John Adams was born near Boston to a prominent family that included direct descendants of Puritans from England. He attended Harvard University and became a lawyer. In 1764 he married Abigail Smith. As a young lawyer, he agreed to defend the British soldiers on trial for killing five Boston residents in an emotional incident that became known as the "Boston Massacre." It was not a popular decision for him, and his law practice suffered as a result. But **Adams believed that those accused of a crime had the right to defend themselves in court.**

Adams's belief in fairness and justice made people respect him, and he became more interested in politics. He became a vocal opponent of the Stamp Act and quickly took up the patriot cause. He was elected to the Massachusetts Assembly and was a delegate to the First Continental Congress. In 1776, along with Thomas Jefferson and two other delegates, he helped draft the Declaration of Independence. In 1777 he served as the head of the Board of War and Ordnance. And in 1783 he helped negotiate the Treaty of Paris with Benjamin Franklin and John Jay.

When George Washington was elected president in 1789, Adams served as vice president for Washington's two terms. Then, in 1796, he ran for president and won against Thomas Jefferson. He died on July 4, 1826, the same day as Thomas Jefferson, fifty years after the signing of the Declaration of Independence. John Adams's son, John Quincy Adams, went on to become the sixth president of the United States.

John Adams was the first president to actually live in the White House. He moved in before it was completely finished.

THE PARIS TREATY

PROTECTORS OF LIBERTY:

Building a New Government

Once the Declaration of Independence was signed and sent to King George III, it was time to start forming a new central government that connected the thirteen independent states. But first they needed a document that would explain how the new government would be run.

ARTICLES OF CONFEDERATION—RATIFIED MARCH 1, 1781

John Dickinson and a committee of thirteen men wrote what became known as the Articles of Confederation, the first Constitution of the United States. The Articles of Confederation named the union of states the United States of America. It was ratified (approved) on March 1, 1781. Under the Articles of Confederation, each state was independent. They could and should govern themselves. However, it also established a federal government. Congress kept the sole right to make treaties and alliances with other nations, maintain a strong military, create a postal service, and coin the money that every state would eventually use.

JOHN DICKINSON

(1732–1808)

"Penman of the Revolution" and Author of the Articles of Confederation

John Dickinson was born on a tobacco farm in Maryland and later moved to Delaware with his family. He was a spirited boy who excelled in school. He married Mary Norris and became a lawyer in Philadelphia. As his legal reputation grew, he felt a pull to enter politics. He was elected to the Delaware legislature and then the Pennsylvania assembly. During those years, the tension between the colonies and the king over taxes and unjust laws was increasing.

In the mid-1760s, Dickinson wrote twelve very popular articles in the *Pennsylvania Chronicle* that attacked the harsh taxes the king was forcing on the colonies. The articles encouraged the people to resist while suggesting that a peaceful outcome was still possible.

Dickinson attended the First Continental Congress in 1774 and the Second Continental Congress in 1775–76. **As a delegate from Pennsylvania, he helped write a document that explained why the colonies felt it was time to move from words to weapons in their fight against the king.** At the same time, he worked on the Olive Branch Petition, a final attempt to peacefully end the conflict.

In June 1776, Congress selected a committee to write a legal document that would oversee the country while it was at war with Great Britain. Dickinson was chosen as committee chairman to write what became known as the Articles of Confederation. After many stops and starts, it was finally approved in 1781.

In 1787, the state of Delaware sent him to the Constitutional Convention. Because of ill health, he had to leave before he could sign the new Constitution. John Dickinson's friend, George Read, signed the Constitution for him. Dickinson died in 1808.

CONSTITUTIONAL CONVENTION—1787

The Articles of Confederation had served as a bridge for governing during the Revolutionary War, but it was by no means perfect. It did not give Congress enough power to collect money from the states, regulate trade, or solve disputes between the states. A new document was needed, one that gave the central government more power. Once again, the states sent delegates to another meeting, the Constitutional Convention, which was held in Philadelphia in the summer of 1787.

James Madison was the first to arrive in Philadelphia for the Constitutional Convention. While he and the other delegates from Virginia waited for the other delegates to arrive, they worked on a new constitution. Most of the ideas were Madison's, coming from his research on other known forms of government. They called their work the Virginia Plan.

Virginia Plan
Louisiana
Purchase

JAMES MADISON

(1751–1836)

"Father of the Constitution" and Fourth President of the United States

James Madison was born in Virginia to a wealthy and important landowning family. After college, he focused his attention on the rising tension between Great Britain and the colonies. Madison served in the Virginia legislature and was a delegate to the Second Continental Congress. A hard worker and a careful speaker, he was brilliant in how he promoted his ideas. He soon earned the reputation as **a master of compromise.** He pushed for a Constitutional Convention and helped persuade George Washington to attend. During the Constitutional Convention, Madison's Virginia Plan was quickly embraced by everyone who read it. Although there was plenty of debate, many compromises, and extensive changes, his plan became the outline for the new constitution. **Madison worked hard to ensure that the new Constitution was ratified by the states.** He wrote articles that

The US Constitution was written on four pages of parchment. It is 4,400 words long and was signed by thirty-nine men. It is the oldest constitution in the world.

explained how a strong central government with many checks and balances was the best way to govern a nation of individual states. Madison's leadership in the drafting process earned him the title of "Father of the Constitution."

In 1789, Madison was elected to the House of Representatives He fulfilled a promise made to Thomas Jefferson and introduced the Bill of Rights, the first amendments to the Constitution. And as Jefferson's secretary of state, he oversaw the complex negotiations for the Louisiana Purchase. **In 1808, he was elected the fourth President of the United States**. After his second term as president, Madison retired to his Montpelier plantation in Virginia and died there in 1836.

It wasn't easy writing a new Constitution. Many people had different ideas about the best way to govern a growing nation that was spread out over a lot of land. When it came to the issue of how to divide power among the states, not just at the present moment but also any that would join the union in the future, the delegates were at an *impasse* (stalemate). Luckily, Roger Sherman, a delegate from Connecticut, came up with a brilliant solution that everyone could agree on.

A New Yorker named Gouverneur Morris wrote the preamble (introduction) to the Constitution:

> "We the People of the United States, in Order to form a more perfect Union, establish Justice, insure domestic Tranquility, provide for the common defense, promote the general Welfare, and secure the Blessings of Liberty to ourselves and our Posterity, do ordain and establish this Constitution for the United States of America."

THE SHORTEST AND TALLEST PRESIDENTS, MADISON AND LINCOLN.

James Madison was the smallest president, at 5 feet 4 inches tall and weighing 100 pounds. Abraham Lincoln was the tallest president at 6 feet 4 inches. The heaviest president was William Howard Taft, weighing in at 332 pounds.

The Continental Association
The Declaration of Independence
The Articles of Confederation
The Constitution

ROGER SHERMAN

(1721–1793)

Delegate to the Constitutional Convention, Author of "The Great Compromise," and Statesman

Roger Sherman was born near Boston, Massachusetts in 1721. As the son of a farmer, he had some schooling but was mostly self-educated. He moved to Connecticut as a young man and married Elizabeth Hartwell. Sherman passed the bar exam to become a lawyer, despite not having any formal education in the law. He served as a judge and on the Connecticut General Assembly. Later he served in the First and Second Continental Congress. But it was at the Constitutional Convention that he played a key role.

The delegates who were writing the Constitution were deadlocked about an important issue. **How would power be divided up between large states and small states?** While large states had more land, they didn't necessarily have more people living there. The smaller states tended to have a larger population. **Sherman and another delegate, Oliver Ellsworth came up with a brilliant solution, what came to be called "The Great Compromise."** They proposed that Congress be made up of two houses: the Senate and the House of Representatives. Each state would elect two members to the Senate, regardless of the size or population. However, states would elect members to the House of Representatives in proportion to the size of their population. This was called a *bicameral* (two house) legislature. The delegates agreed, and Sherman and Ellsworth's idea became the basis for the *legislative* (lawmaking) branch of the US government. Sherman signed the Constitution and made sure that his state of Connecticut supported it by writing newspaper articles under a *pseudonym* (pen name).

Roger Sherman wrote almanacs (reference books) with detailed information about astronomy, religion, and the weather.

Later Sherman served in both houses of Congress as representative in the House of Representatives and as a senator in the Senate. He was able to see how his brilliant compromise worked in real life!

The new Constitution of the United States of America called for a president to be elected. When it came time to select a president, General George Washington, who had led the states to victory in the Revolutionary War and had presided over the Constitutional Convention, was the natural choice.

GEORGE WASHINGTON

(1732–1799)

"Father of His Country," Commander in Chief of the Continental Army, and First President of the United States

George Washington was born in Virginia and spent his youth on Ferry Farm, near Fredericksburg. Washington had only a few years of formal education, but he was good at math. When he was sixteen, he was hired by Lord Fairfax, one of the most powerful men in Virginia, to work as a land surveyor. When his beloved half-brother Lawrence died, Washington inherited Mount Vernon, a place he would call home for the rest of his life.

George Washington owned several sets of false teeth.

He married a wealthy widow named Martha Dandridge Custis and became a member of the Virginia House of Burgesses. By the early 1770s, he was an experienced leader and an emerging voice against the British king. Washington served as a delegate from Virginia in the First and Second Continental Congresses. After the battles at Lexington and Concord in 1775, Congress asked him to lead the Continental Army. Six years later, he accepted the surrender of the British at Yorktown, Virginia.

After the war was over, a group of his officers wanted to declare him king. But he did not want another king for the colonies. In 1787, he was asked to be president of the Constitutional Convention. After the Constitution was signed and ratified, **Washington was elected the first president of the United States and was called the "Father of His Country."** As he rode into Philadelphia on Inauguration Day in 1789, people lined the streets, calling his name and throwing flowers. This amazing transfer of power started our nation on its journey toward "a more perfect union."

MARTHA WASHINGTON

MOUNT VERNON

During his two terms as president, Washington was very aware of the example he was setting for future presidents. By refusing a third term, he signaled that limits should be set on the power of the presidency. He retired to Mount Vernon and died on December 14, 1799.

As president, George Washington had a lot of positions to fill with smart people who could help him run the government. Washington knew that the new court system would be watched by many people to see how the fledgling democracy would operate. For this branch of the government, he needed a person who was up to the task, and he found him in John Jay.

In 1976, Washington was named General of the Armies of the United States. This is the highest rank that anyone in the United States can attain. No one will ever outrank him.

JAY TREATY
AMERICA

JOHN JAY
(1745–1829)

First Chief Justice of the Supreme Court, Author of the Treaty of Paris, and a Contributor to The Federalist Papers

John Jay was born in New York City in 1745 and became a successful lawyer at a young age. He was a delegate at the First and Second Continental Congress. Jay helped negotiate the Treaty of Paris in 1783 that brought an end to the Revolutionary War.

Later, as foreign affairs secretary, Jay became frustrated with the limited power of the central government and pushed for writing a new Constitution. **The new union was in danger of breaking apart and Jay believed that a strong central government would act in the best interests of the country.** Along with Alexander Hamilton and James Madison, he wrote essays that explained how the new government would work and why the state of New York should agree to the new Constitution. This collection of essays became known as ***The Federalist Papers.*** Today they are considered the best work on the nature and role of the Constitution in American life. Though written in 1777 and 1778, *The Federalist Papers* are still consulted and quoted by federal judges when they want to clarify important points in the Constitution.

In 1789, George Washington appointed Jay as the Supreme Court's first *chief justice* (lead judge). Because this was the first time anyone had held this position, **Jay worked hard to establish rules, procedures, and *precedents* (models) for judges that would come after him. In 1795 he worked on a new treaty with Great Britain that is credited with avoiding another war between the countries.** It became known as the Jay Treaty and set a precedent for governments to settle disputes through a process called arbitration.

Jay later became the second governor of New York and ran for president but lost. He retired to his farm and died in 1829.

The John Jay College of Criminal Justice, in New York City, is named after the statesman who played many roles in the young country.

ALLIANCE FOR JUSTICE:

Standing Up for Citizens' Rights

Even after much hard work and many compromises, the Constitution still was not complete. Leaders in the states saw many flaws that had to be fixed. The key issue was that the Constitution did not include protection for individual rights. It mainly addressed how the states and the central government would run the country. But leaders from several states wanted to make sure that individual rights would not get trampled on by the government. They believed that certain freedoms were *inalienable* (guaranteed). Just like people have the right to breathe air, they also have other rights based solely on the fact that they are alive. Those inalienable rights had to be protected so no government could ever take them away. A Bill of Rights was needed, but it would take four more years after ratifying the Constitution, and several visionary men, to create it.

THE BILL OF RIGHTS—1791

Because Congress did not think it had the authority to change the original wording of the Constitution, the only way to fix it was to add *amendments* (revisions) at the end. After much debate, Congress approved ten amendments to the Constitution, and these are known as the "Bill of Rights." They set limits on government power. The founders believed that government could not intrude on people's natural rights, such as the right to speak freely, assemble in groups, be secure in their homes, and worship as they please.

Thomas Jefferson argued, "A bill of rights is what the people are entitled to against every government on earth, general or particular, and what no just government should refuse."

Bill of Rights
SLAVERY

GEORGE MASON

(1725–1792)

"Father of the Bill of Rights"

George Mason was born on a plantation in Virginia and was largely self-educated. As a neighbor of George Washington, he took a keen interest in politics. Like everyone living in the colonies, Mason was aware of the building tension between Great Britain and the colonies. In July 1774, he wrote the Fairfax Resolves, which stated that Virginia rejected the authority of King George III and Parliament. George Washington took the document to the Virginia House of Burgesses and then to the Continental Congress.

From 1775 to 1780, Mason served in the newly renamed Virginia House of Delegates. He led the formation of the new state government and wrote its Constitution and Declaration of Rights. His state's Declaration of Rights was copied by other colonies and became a model for the wording in the Declaration of Independence.

Mason later served as a delegate to the Constitutional Convention in 1787. Many of the phrases in the Constitution can be linked to documents he wrote. **He objected to the powers that were being granted to the new government and was outspoken in his belief that a Bill of Rights was needed.** He also wanted an immediate end to the slave trade. He lost his battle for both that year.

Mason was one of three men who refused to sign the Constitution because it did not include a Bill of Rights. However, his efforts strongly influenced James Madison, who introduced a Bill of Rights at the First Constitutional Congress in 1789. In 1791 the Bill of Rights was finally ratified. George Mason, satisfied that the rights of the individual had been protected at last, died less than a year later.

THE BILL OF RIGHTS

The First Amendment protects freedom of religion, speech, press, assembly, and the right to protest.

The Second Amendment protects a person's right to own a gun.

The Third Amendment protects against soldiers entering a home during war or peace without the homeowner's permission.

The Fourth Amendment protects against unreasonable and unlawful search and seizure of property.

The Fifth Amendment guarantees the right to a fair and legal trial. It also protects someone from testifying against him- or herself under oath.

The Sixth Amendment guarantees anyone accused of a crime a speedy and public trial by jury.

The Seventh Amendment guarantees the right to a trial by jury in civil, or private, legal cases where damages are more than twenty dollars. Civil cases solve disputes between citizens.

The Eighth Amendment prohibits unreasonable bail, excessive fines, and cruel and unusual punishments.

The Ninth Amendment recognizes that citizens have rights that are not listed in the Constitution.

The Tenth Amendment says that the powers not given to the United States government by the Constitution belong to the states or to the people.

The Constitution and the Bill of Rights left one important question unanswered. Who has the right to vote? The Constitution by its silence gave that choice to the states.

In the beginning, the states allowed only white men who owned property to vote. That meant that they had control over every law that was written. By 1856, the property requirement was gone, but still only white men could vote.

The next changes came at a higher price and because the people demanded them. Four amendments were passed through Congress and ratified. Each one gave the right to vote to those who were denied based on their race, skin color, or previous life as a slave (1870); gender (1920); ability to pay taxes (1964); or age (1971).

EMANCIPATION PROCLAMATION AND THE AMERICAN CIVIL WAR—1861 TO 1865

With the words "all men are created equal" ringing in their ears, the founding fathers wrestled with the place slavery held in society. Many of them owned slaves, but they hated the institution of slavery. The southern colonies depended on slave labor for their income. And deep-rooted prejudice was woven into every segment of colonial society. Unfortunately, a choice was made. The issue of slavery was ignored so the bigger issue of unifying the colonies and gaining independence could move forward.

The United States gained huge swaths of land from Great Britain and then purchased more from France. As people moved west, territories were organized and more states wanted to enter the Union. By the time the last founding father died, slavery was gone in the northern states, but it was thriving in the southern states. The question of slavery began to tear the Union apart. Should it be allowed to expand into the new territories? Should it be legal when a territory became a state? The northern states said no, but the southern states said yes.

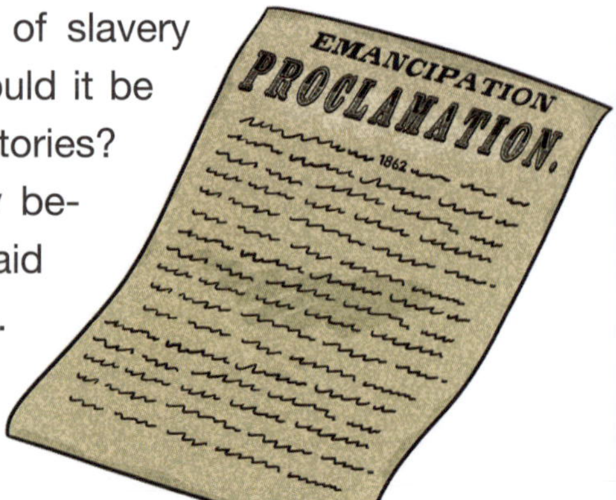

By the start of the Civil War in 1861, the United States had grown to thirty-four states. The battle lines were drawn when seven southern states left the Union and formed their own country, the Confederate States of America. Outgoing Democratic president James Buchanan and incoming Republican president Abraham Lincoln rejected each state's withdrawal, stating emphatically that it was rebellion and illegal.

Confederate forces attacked the Union fortress of Fort Sumter, in South Carolina, on April 12, 1861. President Lincoln was forced to respond and the Civil War began. Two years later, he signed an order called the Emancipation Proclamation. It stated that all slaves in the rebellious states were free. The order changed the reason for the war from preserving the Union to include the end of slavery.

A federal ban on importing slaves was passed in 1808, but the number of slaves in the country grew through increasing birth rates.

Emancipation
Proclamation
FREEDOM

ABRAHAM LINCOLN

(1809–1865)

Author of the Emancipation Proclamation and 16th President of the United States

Abraham Lincoln was born in a one-room log cabin in Kentucky. He had little formal schooling, but he loved to read. He educated himself by reading every book he could find. He became a lawyer and moved to Springfield, Illinois, where he married Mary Todd. He also ran for public office, and served four terms in the Illinois House of Representatives.

He served in the House of Representatives and then won the Republican nomination for a US Senate seat in 1858. In his famous acceptance speech, he said:

> "**A house divided against itself cannot stand.** I believe this government cannot endure permanently half slave and half free."

Although he lost that election, his powerful debates with Stephen Douglas led to his election as president in 1860.

Lincoln inherited a deeply divided nation. As southern states began to leave the Union, Lincoln had to take a stand. The Civil War began in 1861 and Lincoln served as a wartime president for his entire first four-year term. On January 1, 1863, Lincoln used his wartime power as commander in chief to issue the Emancipation Proclamation. **In a swipe of his pen, he freed every slave living in the southern states.** This act added the end of slavery to the war's goals, increased the number of men available to fight, and gained much-needed support from European countries.

Can a state leave the Union? In the 1869 Supreme Court case of Texas v. White, it was determined that no state can leave the Union without the consent of all the other states. The United States is a lasting and unbreakable union.

NANNY AND NANKO, LINCOLN'S BELOVED GOATS.

Abraham Lincoln loved animals and adopted two goats, Nanny and Nanko. They had the run of the White House, something that upset the staff but entertained his sons.

Lincoln won reelection in 1864. In his second inaugural address, he encouraged the former Confederate states to stop fighting and rejoin the Union as quickly as possible.

On April 14, 1865, Lincoln attended a play at Ford's Theater in Washington. An actor named John Wilkes Booth entered the president's state box and shot him. Lincoln died the next day. Booth was captured and killed nearly two weeks later.

THE THIRTEENTH AND FOURTEENTH AMENDMENTS—1865 TO 1877

The Union won the war, but at a great price. More than 620,000 lives were lost and the government spent over 5 billion dollars. Those costs did not include the damage to property mostly in the southern states. Entire cities were burned to the ground. Homes were destroyed. And the southern economy was in ruins. It would take decades to recover.

The Emancipation Proclamation gave southern slaves their freedom. But what about the slaves in the border states and those who fled to the North during the war? There wasn't a law that freed them. And President Lincoln worried that any law Congress passed could be changed in the future. A constitutional amendment was the only way to permanently and forever end slavery.

Congress agreed and passed the Thirteenth Amendment. It made slavery illegal in every state, but left the fate of black civil rights to the states. Many members of Congress worried that this would soon become a problem. And they were right!

Throughout the South, lawmakers began punishing free blacks by writing laws called Black Codes. By passing these laws, southern whites were returning blacks to their prewar slave state.

Congress tried to solve the problem by passing the Civil Rights Act of 1866. It guaranteed citizenship and equal protection under the law regardless of race, skin color, or previous life as a slave. Many congressmen argued that another constitutional amendment was needed.

Black Codes tried to restrict where blacks could travel. They banned them from owning land or guns, forced them into long-term labor contracts, and prevented them from suing or testifying in court.

14th Amendment

JOHN BINGHAM
(1815–1900)
Statesman and Lead Author of the Fourteenth Amendment

John Bingham was born in Pennsylvania in 1815. While he was growing up he observed the evils of slavery and felt it needed to be *abolished* (stopped). He studied to be a lawyer and became active in local politics. From 1857 until 1863 he served in the House of Representatives, where he strongly supported legislation to end slavery and to keep the Union together.

In 1865, he was selected as one of nine men to serve on a committee that would decide how the South would rebuild itself after the Civil War. This period of time, from 1865 until 1877, was called Reconstruction. Important questions needed to be answered. How would the nation cope with the devastation from the war? How would the South's economy function without the work of slaves? How would former slaves be integrated into society? And how would the Union respond to the southern states using Black Codes to keep blacks essentially still in slavery?

In 1866, John Bingham introduced a proposal that became the basis for the Fourteenth Amendment to the Constitution. The amendment secured equal protection under the law for all people in all states. But it stopped short at granting blacks the right to vote. The amendment became part of the Constitution on July 9, 1868.

After Bingham retired from political life, he continued to speak out for equal rights as the South enacted more laws to deprive blacks of equal protection. He died in 1900.

After Lincoln was assassinated, Bingham served on the team of lawyers that prosecuted the people that helped John Wilkes Booth commit his crime.

It took more than passing laws to give blacks their freedom and dignity. It required changing people's hearts and minds about the inherent value of all people. That required passionate dedication and the willingness to speak out in the face of danger and hostility. Only a former slave could truly convince others about the evils of slavery, and only someone who was expressive and educated would be listened to. Those two essential traits came together in Frederick Douglass, a former slave who taught himself to read and write and who risked his life to gain his freedom and secure the rights of others.

After Lincoln was assassinated, Bingham served on the team of lawyers that prosecuted the people that helped John Wilkes Booth commit his crime.

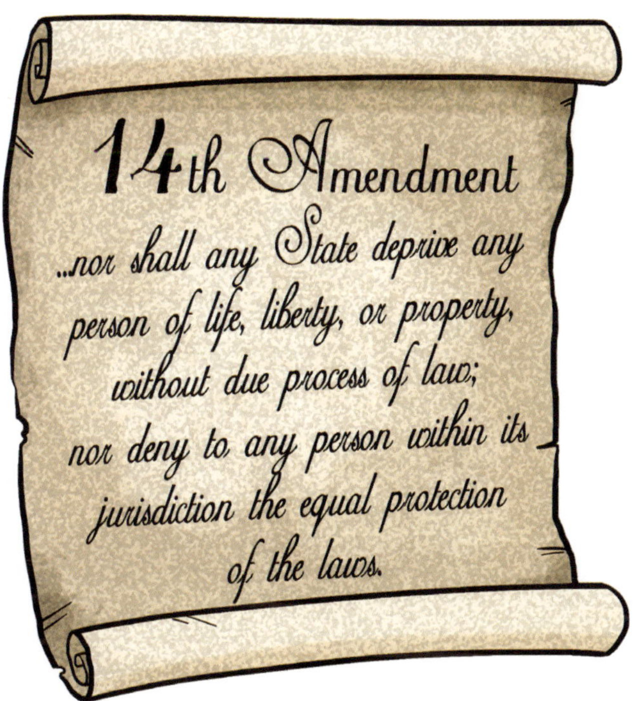

EQUALITY

FREDERICK DOUGLASS

BORN FREDERICK BAILEY (1818–1895)

Antislavery Writer, Publisher, and Speaker

Frederick Bailey's early years were spent living with his grandmother in a shack on a plantation in Maryland. His mother lived on another plantation, and he never knew his father. At age eleven, he became a slave for the Auld family.

Sophia Auld noticed that he was smart and began to teach him the alphabet. When her husband found out, he lectured her on the dangers of teaching slaves to read. She stopped teaching Bailey, but he quietly taught himself with the help of white children he met on the streets and by reading everything he could find.

When he was older, his owner sent him to work for other farmers. **Wherever he went, he tried to teach other slaves to read.** He also tried to escape, but was always caught and returned to his owner. At sixteen, he was sent to a "slave breaker," who used whipping, long hours of work, and fear to destroy the will of unruly slaves.

In 1837, he met a free black woman named Anna Murray who helped him escape to New York City. Once there, he declared himself a free man. Bailey married Murray and they changed their last name to Douglass.

Douglass became a preacher and spoke at meetings and in churches throughout the East and Midwest condemning slavery. In 1847, he started his own newspaper, *The North Star*. **His articles, public speeches, and books made him a leading voice against slavery.** He was often physically and verbally attacked for his views.

After the Civil War broke out, Douglass felt strongly that black men had the right to fight for their freedom. He recruited men for the Massachusetts Fifty-Fourth Regiment for black soldiers. About two hundred thousand black men served in the war, and almost forty thousand died.

Douglass continued to travel and speak on racial issues. **His work helped pass the Fourteenth Amendment and, two years later, the Fifteenth Amendment that gave black men the right to vote.**

In the 1880s, he served in two government positions, and wrote several books that today are considered American autobiography classics. He died in 1895.

Frederick Douglass wasn't the only black person to speak out against slavery. Many people were advocating for an end to it as well. One of the most influential was Mary Ann Shadd Cary, a vocal abolitionist who started her own newspaper for the purpose of helping African Americans and fugitive slaves.

The Provincial Freeman

MARY ANN SHADD CARY

(1823–1893)

Abolitionist and first female African American newspaper editor in North America

Mary Ann Shadd Cary was born into a free African-American family in Delaware in 1823. Her father worked for the anti-slavery newspaper *The Liberator,* which was run by famous *abolitionist* (opponent of slavery) William Lloyd Garrison. Her parents were also part of the Underground Railroad, helping escaped slaves get to freedom in the North. Her home was often used to hide runaway slaves.

Shadd Cary was deeply influenced by this and later became an activist and abolitionist herself. She attended a Quaker school (Quakers were deeply opposed to slavery as well) and later became a teacher. In 1850, Congress passed the Fugitive Slave Act. This law denied runaway slaves the right to a trial by jury and created harsh punishments for people trying to help *fugitive* (runaway) slaves. Shadd Cary and her family moved to Canada to avoid the law and continue their abolitionist activities. In Canada, Shadd Cary started a newspaper called the *Provincial Freemen*. **She wrote articles encouraging blacks and escaped slaves to move to Canada.** She taught fugitive slaves and traveled widely in the United States and Canada, speaking out against slavery at great risk to her own safety.

Later, when the Civil War started, Shadd Cary returned to the United States to help recruit men for the Union Army. **She encouraged African Americans to join the fight against slavery.** As she grew older, she turned her attention to the *suffrage* (women's right to vote) movement. She studied law at Howard University and at age sixty became one of the first black female lawyers in the United States. Mary Ann Shadd Cary died in 1893.

After the Fourteenth Amendment was passed, it became clear that giving blacks their civil rights was not enough. They needed political rights, too. They needed a say in what laws were written and how the government was run. They needed the right to vote.

FIFTEENTH AMENDMENT—1870

After much debate, the Fifteenth Amendment was ratified on February 3, 1870. It said that no one could be denied the right to vote based on their race or skin color. It was specifically written to expand voting rights to black men.

Women had to wait another fifty years after the Fifteenth Amendment was passed to get the right to vote.

DEFENDERS OF EQUALITY:

Fighting for Women's Rights

The Fifteenth Amendment, which gave black men the right to vote, did not apply to women. In the early to mid-1800s, women were still second-class citizens. They had little control over their lives and were seldom sent to school. There were few career options for them except low-paying jobs like nursing and factory work. With the dedication and hard work of many courageous women, though, that was about to change.

AIN'T I
A WOMAN?
SEGREGATION
THUNK!

SOJOURNER TRUTH

BORN ISABELLA BAUMFREE (1797–1883)

Human Rights Advocate

Isabella Baumfree was born a slave in New York. As a child, she didn't know how to read or write and was sold four times to different owners. When Isabella was about thirty years old, she got fed up with life as a slave. With her infant daughter Sophia in her arms, she traveled to New York City and settled there. Sadly, she was forced to leave her other children behind.

In 1843, she had a religious experience that changed her life. She became a preacher and changed her name to Sojourner Truth. **Her new purpose in life was to end the injustices she saw in society.** She traveled across the northern states, speaking whenever and wherever people would listen. And she wrote her autobiography, *"The Narrative of Sojourner Truth: A Northern Slave."*

At almost six feet tall, Truth was a beautiful woman with a deep voice that could capture any audience. **As an ex-slave, she spoke against slavery. As a woman, she spoke for women's rights. And as a human being, she demanded prison reform, an end to capital punishment, and equal justice for everyone.**

In 1851, Truth attended a women's rights convention in Akron, Ohio. Her "Ain't I a Woman?" speech is considered one of the most famous women's rights speeches in American history.

> "Look at me! Look at my arm! I have ploughed and planted, and gathered into barns, and no man could head me! And ain't I a woman?"

During the Civil War, she moved to Washington, DC and worked at the Freedman's Village, helping former slaves who fled to safety there. After the war, she worked for the Freedman's Bureau. She helped former slaves find jobs and settle into life after slavery. She lobbied Congress to stop segregation laws and to give former slaves free land out west.

Truth started a revolution in the hearts of women that compelled them to demand the right to vote and have a voice in their own futures. She died in 1883.

The women's movement officially began in 1848 when Lucretia Mott, Martha Wright, and Elizabeth Cady Stanton organized the first women's rights convention. It was held in Seneca Falls, New York, on July 19 and 20. At the convention, Stanton wrote a Declaration of Rights and Sentiments that demanded women get rights equal to those of men. It called for equal protection under the law, equal education opportunities, the right to own property, and the right to vote.

One woman inspired by the early women's movement was Susan B. Anthony. She traveled around the country giving speeches and organizing local women's rights groups. She was a voice for women of her generation and a symbol of freedom to future generations.

19th
Amendment
VOTE

SUSAN B. ANTHONY
(1820–1906)
"Mother of the Women's Movement"

Susan B. Anthony was born in Massachusetts into a Quaker family well known for their efforts to end slavery. The Anthony home was a Sunday gathering place for activists, including William Lloyd Garrison, the editor of the abolitionist newspaper *The Liberator,* and Frederick Douglass.

Anthony's interest in the women's movement began when she met Elizabeth Cady Stanton. However, it was Lucy Stone's speech at the 1852 Syracuse National Women's Rights Convention that got Anthony excited about helping the cause. **She began to speak at meetings, collect signatures on petitions, and lobby the state legislature for women's property rights and voting rights.**

In 1868, Anthony and Stanton founded the American Equal Rights Association and started its newspaper, *The Revolution*. The next year, **Anthony, Stanton, and a lot of other women joined forces and organized the National Woman Suffrage Association.** Their focus was solely on passing a constitutional amendment giving women the right to vote.

In 1872, Anthony and her three sisters voted in the presidential election. She was arrested and put on trial. In an illegal move, the judge ordered the jury to find her guilty and then he gave her a one hundred dollar fine. Anthony refused to pay. Unfortunately, the judge did not sentence her to prison, so she did not have a chance to appeal the ruling. An appeal would have allowed her to bring her "right to vote" case before the Supreme Court.

Susan B. Anthony died in 1906. When the Nineteenth Amendment giving women the right to vote was finally ratified in 1920, it was called the Susan B. Anthony Amendment as a tribute to her hard work and courage. The Susan B. Anthony coin was made as a tribute to her.

The fight for a woman's right to vote was a long and difficult battle. After the Fifteenth Amendment was ratified, the movement gained strength. The leaders worked at every level of government. They petitioned within each state, trying to gain the right to vote in local and state elections. They filed lawsuits saying that the Fourteenth Amendment applied to women because they were citizens of the United States just like men. And on the national level, they pushed for a constitutional amendment.

NINETEENTH AMENDMENT—1920

By the end of the nineteenth century, women were going to school and entering college in increasing numbers. Across the country, women's rights conventions were challenging the way society viewed them. By the early twentieth century, women could vote in local elections in many states.

Finally, in 1920, the Nineteenth Amendment gave women the right to vote. On Election Day later that year, millions of American women exercised their right to vote for the first time. Their participation in the election process has changed the course of history. But it took decades of hard work and the courage and optimism of many women to make it happen. Elizabeth Cady Stanton was one of the early leaders whose passion and vision helped advance the cause.

The Susan B. Anthony one dollar coin was minted from 1979 to 1981.

WOMEN'S
RIGHTS

ELIZABETH CADY STANTON

(1815–1902)

Early Leader in the Women's Rights Movement and Author of the Declaration of Sentiments

Elizabeth Cady Stanton was the daughter of a lawyer father who made it clear he would have preferred her to be a son. As a young woman, she was drawn to the abolitionist and women's rights movements. In 1840, she married Henry Stanton in a ceremony where she had the word "obey" removed from her wedding vows, a radical act at the time. They settled in Seneca Falls, New York.

In 1848, with Lucretia Mott and Martha Wright, she organized the famous Seneca Falls Convention. At the convention, she took the lead in promoting women's right to vote and authored the Declaration of Sentiments. It was based on the Declaration of Independence and outlined the rights that American women were entitled to as citizens.

When the Declaration of Sentiments was published, many people—men and women—were opposed to its ideas. People's understanding of women's role in society was deeply rooted and hard to change.

Stanton continued to write and lecture about women's rights and became even more outspoken about women's suffrage. After she met Susan B. Anthony in the 1850s, the two began working together. In 1868, they founded *The Revolution*, a weekly paper about women's rights. The two then formed the National Woman Suffrage Association in 1869. Stanton was president of the association for more than twenty years. In her later years, she wrote books detailing the history of the women's suffrage movement. She believed that an amendment to the US Constitution was the only way women would gain the right to vote. She died in 1902, eighteen years too early to see the culmination of her life's work.

Another woman who worked tirelessly to advance the cause of women's suffrage was Carrie Chapman Catt, and she was a key figure in getting the Nineteenth Amendment passed.

LEAGUE of
OTES FOR
WOMEN
Votes
Votes f
WOME

CARRIE CHAPMAN CATT

(1859–1947)

Women's Rights Activist and Founder of the League of Women Voters

Carrie Chapman Catt was born in Wisconsin in 1859. When her father refused to pay for her to go to college, Chapman Catt worked as a teacher to raise the money herself. She attended Iowa State College and then began a career in education and later in newspaper publishing.

In 1887, she became involved in the suffrage movement in Iowa and soon emerged as an important leader. When Susan B. Anthony left her position as president of the National Woman Suffrage Association (now the National American Woman Suffrage Association), Chapman Catt took over. Later, more than ten years after leaving that position, the association fell into disarray. They called Chapman Catt to come back and help them reorganize. It was then that she came up with what became known as the “Winning Plan.” **She decided the organization needed to focus on one goal, and one goal only: winning the women’s right to vote. And she argued that they had to pursue this goal on both the state and national levels.**

Chapman Catt worked tirelessly—organizing, campaigning, getting other women involved, and giving hundreds of speeches. She believed strongly that women should have control over their own lives, and that participating in politics would give them a voice in the decisions that affected them. She founded the League of Women Voters in 1920 to educate and engage women in using their newly won right to vote.

A dynamic leader, Chapman Catt continued to be involved in politics after the Nineteenth Amendment was passed. Unsurprisingly, she turned her attention to helping women in nations around the world gain the right to vote. She died in 1947.

Seven more amendments were passed after women got the right to vote. As society grows and changes, more amendments will come. The Constitution will change and it should change, but only if the people make it happen. Each generation will have to fight to preserve their rights, because in each generation there are people who would happily take them away.

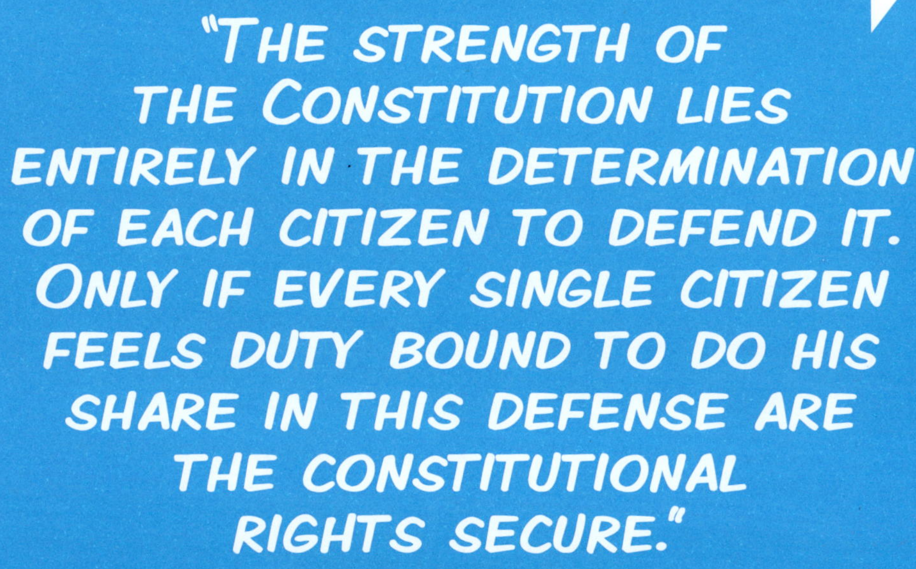
"The strength of
the Constitution lies
entirely in the determination
of each citizen to defend it.
Only if every single citizen
feels duty bound to do his
share in this defense are
the constitutional
rights secure."
—Albert Einstein

CONSTITUTION TIMELINE

1787: Constitution is signed and sent to the states to ratify.

1788: Nine of the thirteen states ratify the Constitution. It becomes the law of the land.

1791: Bill of Rights is ratified.

1795: Eleventh Amendment expands the legal power of the federal courts.

1804: Twelfth Amendment defines how the president and vice president are elected.

1865: Thirteenth Amendment makes slavery illegal.

1868: Fourteenth Amendment says those born or naturalized in the United States, including all former slaves, are citizens and have equal protection under the law.

1870: Fifteenth Amendment says no one can be denied the right to vote based on race or skin color. Specifically grants African-American men the right to vote.

1913: Sixteenth Amendment gives Congress the power to tax a citizen's income.

1913: Seventeenth Amendment changes how US senators are elected—not by state legislatures but by popular vote.

1919: Eighteenth Amendment forbids the manufacture, sale, and transport of liquor.

1920: Nineteenth Amendment gives women the right to vote.

1933: Twentieth Amendment sets January 20 as Presidential Inauguration Day.

1933: Twenty-First Amendment repeals the Eighteenth Amendment. It is again legal to make, sell, and distribute alcohol.

1951: Twenty-Second Amendment sets term limits for the president.

1961: Twenty-Third Amendment gives citizens living in the District of Columbia the right to vote in presidential elections.

1964: Twenty-Fourth Amendment forbids any tax on voting.

1967: Twenty-Fifth Amendment says who is in line to be president if the sitting one dies, resigns, or is not able to perform the duties of president.

1971: Twenty-Sixth Amendment sets the voting age at eighteen for federal elections. It took only one hundred days to ratify.

1992: Twenty-Seventh Amendment defines how Congress can increase their pay. It took more than 203 years to ratify!

GLOSSARY

Amendment: a change in wording or meaning especially in a law, bill, or motion

Cede: to give up or formally surrender to another

Constitution: the structure that defines the values under which a nation is governed

Delegate: a person sent with power to act for another

Draft: a first or early form of any writing, subject to change

Federal: applies to the central government of a union of states, distinct from the individual state governments

Inauguration: a ceremony to mark the formal beginning of something

Judicial: relating to courts of law or to judges

Legislature: an elected group of people who are given the power to make, change, or repeal laws

Litigate: to carry on a lawsuit

Official: a person selected or elected to an office

Opponent: a person who is on an opposite side in a war, game, or conflict; a rival

Parliament: a legislative body; in Great Britain, the House of Lords and the House of Commons

Petition: a request to an authority asking for something, often bears the names of those making the request

Protégé: a person under the care of someone interested in his or her career or welfare

Ratify: to approve by stating agreement

Repeal: to take back or withdraw; to cancel

Representative: a person who speaks for a group of people in a legislative body, especially a member of the US House of Representatives

Revolution: the overthrow of an established government or political system by the people governed

Suffrage: the right to vote, especially in a political election